Lessons

Stephanie McNutt

Presentation by *BookLeaf Publishing*

Web: www.bookleafpub.com

E-mail: info@bookleafpub.com

ISBN: 9789358368154

First edition 2023

To Dallas, for supporting me through my crazy dream and through every moment I veered off my true path.

ACKNOWLEDGEMENT

Thank you so much to all of my friends and family that have supported me through this journey. I could not have done this without friends reminding me to go out and enjoy myself once in a while. Thank you Keith for being patient as I worked on this and missed some skating time. Thank you to my mother-in-law for her steadfast guidance and patience, and to my father-in-law for his quick wit and good hugs. To Aunt Rhonda, thank you for telling me to get over all the fears I had and just write, and reminding me that if I just wrote the thing, I'd have at least one sale from you. I love and miss you so much. Dallas, thank you so much for being my support system, my rock, and my sanity check. I'm sure I could achieve a lot of success on my own, but you give me someone to celebrate it all with, and for that, I am forever grateful. To everyone else I have missed because I have exhausted my brain writing all these poems, thank you. From the bottom of my heart, thank you for your love and support.

INDEX

Stones

I was raised on a diet of stones.
Hard words thrown with
the intention of wounding and bruising,
never letting me forget
my existence is an inconvenience.
Huge bricks used to build towering walls
to keep us separated.
I was a child forced to peer over walls
to see her mother's face.

Trees

So I escaped into two worlds,
both made of trees.
The first a forest of fluttering pages
stories that helped me forget
that I was useless, unwanted, unloved.
Pages that taught me what love really looks like
and that happily ever after exists.
The other was cold and dark,
but just as comforting.
A place to escape from screams and insults
a place that was quiet for the right reasons
a place that I didn't have to calculate how to
move
I could just sit there, listening to the birds live
normal lives
while I escaped into someone else's time.

Brothers

I hope someday my brothers know
I had to leave.
Leaving was survival.
Leaving was escaping another pregnancy I never
asked to have
that someone else had to end to hide their own
sins.
Childhood was supposed to be
sprinklers and popsicles and laughter
but ours was
begging and screaming and crying.
I wanted to take them with me
to end it all for them too,
but I was too young to know how to do
anything,
but old enough to know I needed to run to
survive.

Honor Your Mother

"She's your mother, you can't just leave her,
you're supposed to love her."
Yes.
She was my mother.
She was supposed to love me.
But she didn't.
If there was no public, no convenience, nothing
to gain,
she didn't.
But no one told her,
"But she's your daughter, you're supposed to
love her."

Son

I hope that someday
when you realize the world is unkind
I've done enough to teach you
how to make it kind again.
I hope that someday
I've done enough to change this world
so you don't have to do the same for your
children.
I hope that someday
allowing you to be a sensitive boy
makes you a caring and compassionate man.

Boys Will Be Boys

6

Boys will be boys.
That's what they tell me
every time my son comes home
wet from the creek and leaves in his hair.
I hope I've also taught him that
boys will be kind
boys will be honest
boys will be gentle
boys will be strong
boys will be compassionate
boys will be soft
boys will be loving
boys will be good.

Holding Hands

Every time we cross the street, you hold my
hand.
When you were two,
your dad would hold your other hand
and we'd carry you to the other side
your legs dancing in the air over the crosswalk.
When you turned five,
you'd race across the street
little legs moving as fast as they could to keep
up with mine
not letting go until we got back to the car.
Today you are seven years old
and you let go of my hand halfway through the
crosswalk.
"I can cross by myself, Mom."
How have I missed this slow progression of you
dropping my hand
farther and farther away from the crosswalk?
Will I notice when you hold my hand to cross
the street
for the last time?

Rain

The weatherman calls for rain
so the woods will be empty.
The perfect time for a long walk.
We pull on rubber boots and hooded jackets
and race out the door.
We can't see through the water dripping in our
eyes
but we don't mind.
We can feel the woods around us
like birds flying in familiar skies.

Time Is a Thief

One moment you're coming home
from the hospital
the next that baby is whisked away
and in that place a big kid
too big to hold hands
too big for your lap
too big for help
suddenly you've stopped playing tooth fairy
because the adult teeth are all in
and you're navigating
date nights
and graduation
and moving out
and moving on.

Spring

A breeze ruffles the hair
of suntanned boys rolling down green hills.
Little girls blow dandelion fuzz
spreading wishes and seeds for future flower
crowns.
What was once still is abuzz
flitting from flower to bursting flower,
whispering words of growth and renewal.
Green vines that were still move on again
giving color to gray buildings and wizened trees.
The sun reaches out and touches everyone,
the children, the bees, the flowers, and the
darkest corners of the ground.
The Earth is finally remembering her beauty
again.

Friends

I don't care
if your house is clean.
I do care
if you smile when you open your door.
I care if my difference of opinion
will make me less welcome.
I care if I am welcome at your table
and if you make space for me beside you.

I do not care
if your floor is swept.
I care that you sweep the cobwebs of my heart
from my weariness at the world.
I care about conversations over coffee and
kitchen counter philosophy.

I do not care
if your laundry is folded.
I care if you love me with all my wrinkles and
creases.
I care if you'll help wash away the dirt settled in
my soul.

I do not care
what your home looks like
I do care
what your heart looks like.

Me

And then one day
the girl getting lost in the books
became the girl writing them

The Moon

14

There is no person I wish to imitate
as much as I wish to imitate the moon.
She chooses not to compete with the sun
but shine in her own right.
She manages to inspire painters and poets alike,
even when she is not whole.

Daughter

If I ever have a daughter
I would hope no one ever asks her
if she lost weight.
I hope they have other questions instead.
Questions like,
How is your soul?
What is art to you?
What makes you laugh?
What makes you feel alive?
What occupies your mind when you can't sleep?
Who do you wish to become?

His Mom

You make cookies with my son
and take me out for sweet tea.
The passenger seat of your car is
my church, my therapist's office, my home.
We drive around the dusty town your son was
eager to leave
sharing what makes our soft hearts ache.
Each time I realize how much we are the same
and I cry with joy
knowing I see myself in
someone else for the first time.

You Are My Sun

You are my sun.
But not on a hot summer day.
No, you are my sun after months of
cold gray skies.
When the winter winds whip through
to my bones
and I pray for warmth.
You are the break in the clouds
that lift my face to the sky
and make me sing again.

Love

18

He's grumpy in the mornings
but I know he loves me still.
I hear it in the sound of the tea brewing.
The tea he doesn't drink a drop of
but he makes it anyway.

His Dad

You smell of leather and cigarettes
and never have much to say.
But I could sit in the room with you for hours
basking in the comfortable silence
that brings unspeakable peace.
We laugh at jokes not meant for delicate ears
and ruminate on the state of the world
then fall back into that comfortable silence
that makes me feel like I belong.

Kindness

20

I don't find my greatest peace
in the big moments and grand gestures.
I find faith in the world
in the small acts of kindness and the minor deeds
of strangers and neighbors.
Life is bearable because of the
small everyday acts of humankind
that shine light in the darkness.

Keep Walking

In the midst of darkness
I know there is light.
I know that one cannot exist without the other.
When I take stock of my life
I know that whatever path I am on
the landscape will change
and I will find happiness again
if only I keep walking.

Lessons

The best lesson the sun and moon
taught me
is that I should
shine my own way
and the people meant for me will
stick around and dance in my light.